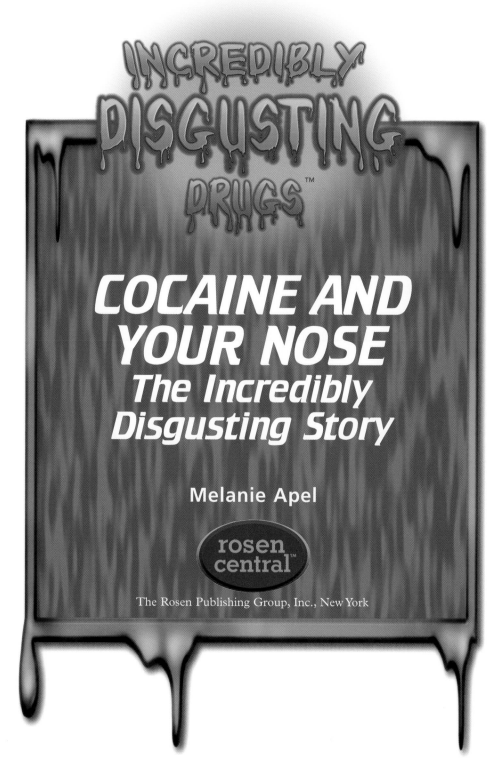

INCREDIBLY DISGUSTING DRUGS™

COCAINE AND YOUR NOSE
The Incredibly Disgusting Story

Melanie Apel

rosen central™

The Rosen Publishing Group, Inc., New York

The author wishes to thank Mindy Apel for her research assistance.

Published in 2000, 2006 by The Rosen Publishing Group, Inc.
29 East 21st Street, New York, NY 10010

Library of Congress Cataloging-in-Publication Data

Apel, Melanie Ann.
Cocaine and your nose: the incredibly disgusting story / Melanie
Ann Apel.
p. cm. — (Incredibly disgusting drugs)
Includes bibliographical references and index.
Summary: Explains the parts and functions of the nose, how the body breathes and smells, the effects of the drug cocaine, and how to get treatment for addiction.
ISBN 1-4042-0632-9 (lib. bdg.)
1. Cocaine—Toxicology—Juvenile literature. 2. Nose—Juvenile literature. 3. Respiratory organs—Juvenile literature. [1. Cocaine. 2. Drug abuse. 3. Nose. 4. Respiratory system.]
I. Title. II. Series.
RA1242.C75 A64 2000
616.86'47—dc21

00-020210

Manufactured in the United States of America

CONTENTS

Introduction: Get On Board!

Hold on to your hats because you're about to go on a wild ride through the human body. Along the way, you'll see some pretty gross pictures and learn some interesting, important, and maybe even life-saving facts. You'll also find out exactly what happens to your body—on the outside and the inside—when you take cocaine.

Cocaine use and addiction continue to be growing problems in America and throughout the world. In 2004, about 35 million Americans ages 12 and older used cocaine at least once. That's more than the population of Texas! Two million Americans use cocaine regularly.

Even though cocaine use has decreased since the mid-1960s, it's becoming popular again, especially among young people. As

Infarction, or blockage in blood circulation, of the human lung is often caused by drug abuse. The areas in red represent damage to the blood cells and lining of the lung. In a healthy lung, these areas would be clear.

cocaine becomes easier and cheaper to obtain, it draws more and more users. In fact, more than half of the high schoolers interviewed in a 2003 survey claimed to have had access to cocaine. That's pretty frightening considering that cocaine is one of the deadliest substances available—it can kill you even if you use it only once.

Directly after taking cocaine in any amount, you greatly increase your risk of having a heart attack. Twenty-five percent of the heart attacks that occur among eighteen- to forty-year-olds are caused by cocaine use.

Cocaine use has many other nasty side effects, including twitching, severe paranoia (a mental disorder in which one feels extreme distrust toward others), splitting headaches, abdominal pain, nausea, brain and lung damage, and breathing problems. Sounds awful, doesn't it? Well, continue reading.

1 Anatomy of a Nose

Your body needs oxygen to live. To get this oxygen, your body uses a process called respiration. Your lungs take in oxygen and pass it to your blood. Your blood then carries the oxygen all over your body, delivering it to your body's tissues and organs. Your lungs also get rid of carbon dioxide, the stale, used air in your body.

Your nose (along with your mouth) is the starting point of the respiratory system. In addition to bringing in fresh oxygen, your nose is responsible for keeping dust and dirt from getting into your body, and for warming and humidifying (moistening) the air you breathe in.

Aside from being a main entrance to your respiratory system and trapping all that dirt and dust, your nose has another important job. It is

Interior Nose Diagram

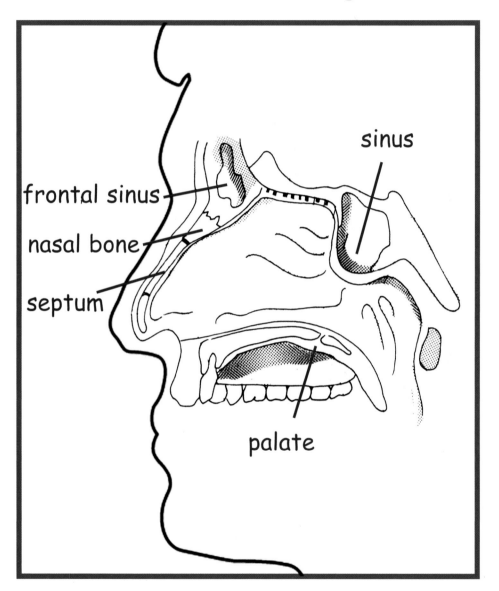

sinus

frontal sinus

nasal bone

septum

palate

the main sense organ involved in smelling. By sniffing out millions of smells around you, your nose gives you very important information about your surroundings. Your nose smells smoke and lets you know that you should escape from a burning house. It tells you that possibly harmful chemicals, like model glue or turpentine, are nearby. The smell of eggs and pancakes can be your wake-up call to breakfast on a lazy Saturday morning. How does your little nose do such an important job, you ask?

WHAT YOUR NOSE IS MADE OF

Let's explore the human nose more closely. Obviously, the outside of your nose is a lot easier to examine than the inside, so let's start with that.

Along with your mouth, your nose is the main entry and exit for air to get to and from your lungs. It is made of two main materials: bone, which is very hard and unbendable, and soft tissue, which is a combination of fat and skin. You will notice that the tip and sides of your nose are softer than the bridge—the long, straight part—of your nose. That's because these parts are made of that soft tissue.

The long, straight part of your nose is made of bone and something called cartilage, which is a special kind of soft tissue that is not as tough as bone but is much sturdier than regular soft tissue.

Looking at the lower part of your nose, you'll see two openings, one on each side. These openings, called nostrils, lead to the deeper, darker, not-so-easily-seen areas of your nose—the nares, or internal pas-

Exterior Nose Diagram

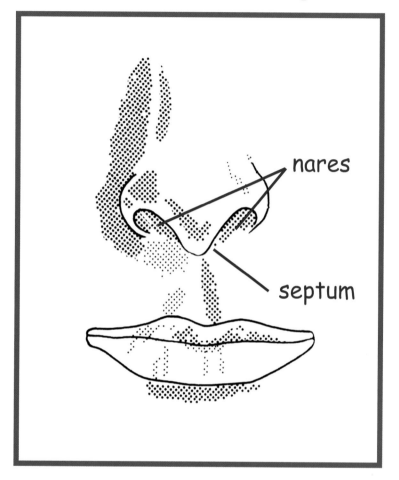

nares

septum

sages. The nares are separated by a piece of bone and cartilage called the septum. The nares lead to the nasal cavity, a chamber (hole) directly behind your outer nose, where the air you breathe in goes to get warm. On both sides of the nasal cavity are smaller chambers called sinuses.

olfactory bulb

The brain's olfactory bulb allows for the detection and interpretation of different smells. Damage to olfactory nerve cells, a frequent result of cocaine use, can permanently destroy one's sense of smell.

The Mucous Membrane

The whole respiratory passageway—from the entrance to the nasal cavity down through your throat and into your lungs—is lined by a mucous membrane that has many special properties. One such property is the ability to sense smells around you and send information about these smells to the brain.

Tiny olfactory hairs on the roof and sides of the nasal cavity are responsible for detecting smells and sending the information to nerve cells on the top of the cavity. From there, the signals are sent to the olfactory bulb and then interpreted by your brain as different smells. (Check out chapter 2 for more details on smelling.)

Another responsibility of the mucous membrane is to detect germs and viruses in your body. When white blood cells in the membrane sense signs of an infection in your body, they call in your body's natural defenses to help get rid of the unwanted visitors.

Don't Forget About Your Throat

Have you ever had the odd experience of taking a sip of milk or soda only to have it come shooting out of your nose? That's because your nose and mouth are connected by your pharynx (the scientific term for throat). Normally, when you drink, your body pushes the liquid down toward your stomach by swallowing. But if there is liquid in your throat that gets pushed upward instead (say, because you sneeze or start laughing really hard in the middle of drinking), the liquid can enter your nose. When that happens, it has nowhere to go but out through your nostrils!

2 The Respiratory and Olfactory Systems

As we saw in chapter 1, your nose, along with your mouth, is the starting point of a very important system in your body—the respiratory system. The respiratory system is the set of organs—including your nose, mouth, and lungs—that enable you to breathe. Air from outside your body gets into your body through your nose. Your nose then performs several very important functions on this air before it enters the rest of your body.

First of all, your nose is responsible for filtering out dirt, dust, pollen, germs, and even tiny insects flying in the air—anything that could make you really sick if your nose weren't there to keep it from getting into your body. How does your nose do this?

There are two main ways that your nose filters the air around you. First, the hairs that line the inner passages of the nose form a barrier to keep out small particles. Your nose's second weapon against unwelcome intruders, believe it or not, is mucus—yep, that slimy stuff that comes out when you blow your nose. Dust, dirt, and other floating particles that we inhale get trapped by the sticky mucus and never get farther into the body. Then, when we blow our noses, these particles get flushed out along with the mucus.

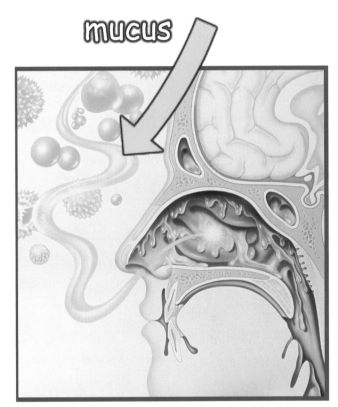

A second important job your nose performs is humidifying and warming the air it brings into your body. All this means is that your nose makes the air moist and

Mucus moistens and protects the respiratory system, filtering dust, dirt, and germs from inhaled air. Cocaine use damages the mucous membrane, leaving the body vulnerable to viral and bacterial infections.

warm before it goes into your body. If your nose didn't do this, breathing air in and out would be pretty uncomfortable because the cold, dry air would be a shock to your system.

Think about what it's like when your nose gets stuffed up from a cold. You have to do all your breathing through your mouth, right? Try this for a minute or two by tightly holding your nose. Is the inside of your mouth starting to feel dry? What about your throat? That's why having a healthy nose to breathe through is so important!

WHAT'S THAT SMELL?

The other job of your nose is to smell things. This has been mentioned already, but let's get into it a little more here. We all know that odors, or smells, come in many different varieties. Some odors, like the smell of Thanksgiving dinner or fresh flowers, are very nice to have around. Others, like your brother's feet, aren't quite as pleasant. Whether you are smelling nice odors or awful ones, your sense of smell is very important in keeping your body safe and healthy. Your sense of smell helps you get important information. For example, smelling a certain type of perfume may let you know that your favorite aunt is somewhere nearby. Sniffing a container of milk can tell you whether it's OK to drink or if you should trash it right away.

For one reason or another, some people don't have as good a sense of smell as other people do. In addition to it being a drag (imagine not being able to smell grape bubble gum or fresh brownies!), having a poor sense of smell can be a real problem. Think about what it would be like if you couldn't count on your nose to tell you important things, such as the fact that the room you are in has been recently painted or that something is burning in the oven. You might end up with some fresh wet paint on your new shirt or, far worse, a house fire.

Super Sniffers

How does a healthy nose sniff out smells? It starts just after air is filtered by the nostrils and is on its way to the lungs through the nasal cavity (right behind your outer nose). On the roof and sides of the nasal cavity, there's a small

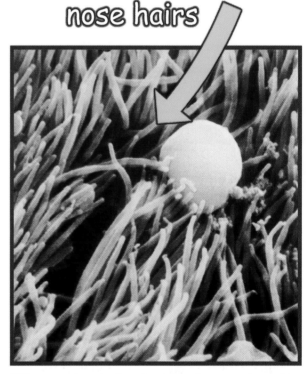

nose hairs

Cilia, or tiny hairs inside the nasal cavity, allow for the transportation of fluids such as mucus throughout the respiratory system.

HOW FAST DO YOU SNEEZE?

Why do you sneeze? When dirt or extra mucus enters your nose, it can irritate the linings of the air spaces inside your nose. This irritation makes you take a deep breath and then blast air through your nose at more than 100 miles (or 161 kilometers) per hour to get rid of the intruder!

area of nerve cells—only about the size of a postage stamp—that start off the smelling process.

If you look at one of these nerve cells under a microscope, you'll see millions of tiny hairlike structures, called cilia, along the edge of the cell. These cells are covered with receptors sensitive to odor particles in the air.

The receptors are your body's private detectives, always on the prowl for smell molecules lurking around your nasal passages. There are around 10 million receptors in your nose, and there are at least twenty different types of receptors. Each type can sense a different range of smell molecules. When one set of receptors senses the presence of smell molecules, those receptors send the information, in the form of nerve signals, along your olfactory (smell) nerve to your brain's smell center.

When new information comes in from the olfactory nerve, the smell center gets busy analyzing the signal pattern and identifying the smell. Based on the information gathered by the cilia and the olfactory nerve, plus what it already knows from past smelling experiences, your brain determines whether the smell is "good" or "bad" and then tells you what the smell is.

Matching a smell to an object or person can happen almost immediately, but sometimes your brain might need a few moments to figure out what you're smelling. Sometimes, of course, your brain doesn't recognize the smell at all, and you are left to guess what the smell is.

YOUR NOSE AND YOUR MEMORY

Have you ever smelled something and immediately felt a strong emotion? The reason we associate smells with events or people is that the part of your brain that is responsible for smelling is also responsible for your emotions and your memory. This part of the brain is called the limbic system (hmmm, let's see—think you can remember that?).

limbic system

The brain's nerve pathways and thalamus, shown in red, allow for the reception of sensory information. These nerves lead into the brain's limbic system, shown in yellow. Damage to this system can interfere with one's ability to recognize pain and emotions.

3 The Real Deal on Cocaine

OK, so we've seen that the nose has some pretty important responsibilities. We've also seen that the way it works is complicated. That means that when you snort cocaine, you could be damaging the system at many different levels. And that means trouble. Keep reading to learn the gory details about what cocaine can do to mess up this fragile system.

WHAT COCAINE CAN DO TO YOUR BODY

When you think of having fun or having a good time, what kinds of activities come to mind? Do you think of watching a movie, going to a party, or hanging out with friends? Or do you prefer going to an amusement park, a football game, or the beach?

People use drugs for lots of different reasons, but one of the most common reasons, especially among young people, is that they think doing drugs is a way of having a good time. Even when kids know that drugs like cocaine can be really dangerous, they never think that those bad things could happen to them.

The problem is, they're wrong. Dead wrong, in fact. Drugs like cocaine can kill anyone, of any age, at any time. Thousands of kids and teens die every year just from trying new drugs once "to see what it's like." Young people with perfectly healthy hearts can die of a heart attack just from using cocaine one time. Cocaine can kill athletes who are in top shape by stopping their breathing.

THE LONG ARM OF THE LAW

In addition to the extremely severe health problems that cocaine can cause, it can also lead to some serious problems with the law. That's because buying, selling, and using cocaine are all illegal.

Does getting caught by the police sound like fun? How about telling your parents that you've been using drugs? In some cases, you may even be sent to jail or be forced to do community service if you are caught possessing cocaine. Although some teens and adults think that doing hard drugs like cocaine is "having a good time," they probably don't feel that way when they wind up in jail.

What would happen if the police caught you using cocaine? First, they'd call your parents and tell them that you'd been using drugs. At your court hearing, depending on your age and the amount of cocaine you were carrying, you might receive a jail sentence that would make your stomach flip. If you're lucky, you would only have to put in many, many hours of community service and take classes that would teach you all about the disgusting effects of cocaine use.

Even when people are aware of the damage that cocaine can cause, they never think that they will be the victim. "I knew that cocaine could kill you, but I never thought it would happen to someone I know," says Kim, aged fourteen. "Shana was only thirteen when she died, and it was her first time taking cocaine." Nobody is safe from the dangers of drugs.

Dealing cocaine or possessing it in large quantities is much more serious and can result in much longer jail sentences. So the next time you're thinking it might be fun to use cocaine, remember that it's no fun winding up in a jail cell like the one above or, even worse, the emergency room.

WHAT IS A DRUG ANYWAY?

A drug is a substance that changes your body's natural chemistry, which in turn can change your mood and behavior. In other words, ingesting drugs can alter the way you normally think, feel, and act. There are many different kinds of drugs, both natural and man-made, that do many different things to the body.

The Different Types of Drugs

So far we've been talking about "hard" drugs, like cocaine, that are illegal to use, sell, and buy. But there are plenty of legal drugs, too. Aspirin and cough medicine are examples of drugs that you can easily buy at the supermarket or drugstore without special permission.

A few drugs are legal for most people but not everyone. In the United States, for example, there are minimum ages for buying and using alcohol and tobacco products (like cigarettes and chewing tobacco), which are considered drugs.

And then there are drugs that are legal to buy, sell, and use but only when a doctor has prescribed them to you. Some common prescription drugs are medications for asthma, antibiotics for infections, and

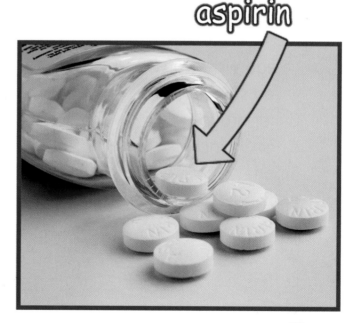

aspirin

painkillers for people who have just had an operation or who have a bad injury.

It's important to know that even though these kinds of drugs are legal, they can be just as dangerous as illegal drugs if they are not used the way they are meant to be used. All drugs can be harmful, including legal drugs that are taken for too long or in too large of a dose, medicines used without a prescription, and illegal drugs used to get high.

Stimulants

As you now know, cocaine is an illegal drug. It is also one of the most addictive substances known to humans. This means that once you start using cocaine, it's really hard to stop.

Cocaine is in a category of drugs called stimulants. Other drugs in this category include amphetamines (also known as pep pills or uppers) and caffeine, which is found in coffee, tea, and chocolate. Strong

cocaine

stimulants like cocaine make your heart beat really fast, sometimes so fast that it gets tired out and stops beating altogether. Stimulants can also make you really nervous and unable to concentrate.

Aside from physically damaging the body, cocaine can also ruin a person's life. Once someone is addicted—and that can happen after the first try—he or she will do anything to get more of the drug. Being addicted to a drug means that you need the drug just to get through each day. This can make you spend all of your money and then steal more; lose your home, job, and family; and go to jail.

Where Does Cocaine Come From?

Cocaine has been around for hundreds of years. Most of it is grown in South American countries like Bolivia and Peru. People who lived there a long time ago used to chew on the leaves of the coca plant because the leaves gave them the energy they needed to work high up in the mountains without much food. They also used the coca leaves in religious ceremonies.

For many years, Native Americans grew mainly vegetable crops and only small numbers of coca plants. Eventually, illegal drug traffickers (people who buy and sell illegal drugs) made the Native Americans stop growing their healthy vegetable crops and grow only coca plants instead. Soon, Native

The coca plant, or *Erythroxylon coca*, is the primary source of cocaine.

Americans learned to mix coca leaves with kerosene and then dry the mixture in the sun to make a yellow paste. When smoked, this paste made the user feel very good. Today, this paste is smoked not only by Native Americans but by people all around the world.

Most of the paste made in Bolivia, Peru, and other nearby countries is sent to Colombia, another country in South America. Colombia is home to the people who control most of the cocaine traffic in the world. They are the ones who make the actual cocaine and then ship it to the United States and other parts of the world, where people use it to get high.

A little more than 200 years ago, that same coca plant found its way to Europe. The first actual cocaine as we know it today was not made until 1855. At that time, cocaine was used as an anesthetic, a drug that makes the body numb

OTHER NAMES FOR COCAINE

Black rock, base, electric Kool-Aid, real tops, roxanne, twinkie, yam, coke, snow, flake, blow, cola, rock, nose candy, toot, white, powder.

and unable to feel pain. But even then, people knew that cocaine could cause pleasure, too. Some people were already taking cocaine for fun.

Since cocaine was cheap and easy to get back then, doctors began giving it to their patients to treat many different health problems. Cocaine was also added as an ingredient in many medicines because patients felt really good after taking it. Of course, what doctors didn't know back then was that this good feeling is only temporary and that cocaine use is actually extremely dangerous. They had no idea that there would be negative side effects to putting so many people on cocaine. As a result, many people ended up with far more serious problems, including addiction and death.

Cocaine and Coca-Cola

Here's a really weird factoid about cocaine: it was an ingredient in the first recipe for Coca-Cola. When Coca-Cola first came out in 1885, it was considered a healthy (!) drink because people felt energized and happy after drinking it. Believe it or not, Coca-Cola contained cocaine for the first twenty years that it was sold.

Cocaine was removed from the drink around 1905, when doctors finally realized that cocaine wasn't good for people. People were getting sick and even dying from taking too much cocaine, so doctors stopped prescribing it, too. Thanks to the Pure Food and Drug Act of 1906, any use of cocaine for nonmedical purposes was declared illegal.

COCAINE IN AMERICA

In the early days, cocaine was cheap and easy to get, but its price eventually went way up and people had to spend a lot more money to get it.

Cocaine was introduced to the United States in the mid-nineteenth century. The coca plant was exported from South America and originally sold as a treatment for fatigue. However, people soon realized that cocaine was destroying their health, and the U.S. government banned the drug in 1914, under the Harrison Tax Act.

Even though cocaine is illegal, people still find ways to get it and use it. Beginning in the 1960s and peaking in the 1980s, there was a huge demand for cocaine and drugs in general. People were using drugs regularly and in greater amounts than ever before.

According to recent studies, most cocaine users are between the ages of eighteen and thirty. However, people from all walks of life use cocaine: rich people, poor people, kids, teenagers, adults, people with lots of education, and others with very little schooling. The important thing to remember about cocaine is that its effects are harmful and sometimes fatal, no matter where you come from or how old you are. Comedian John Belushi, above, died of an overdose of cocaine mixed with heroin when he was just thirty-three. Comedian Chris Farley died of a cocaine and morphine overdose, also when he was thirty-three.

4 Cocaine, Your Nose, and the Rest of Your Body

Cocaine can actually be taken three different ways. It can be smoked, injected, or—the way it affects noses most directly—snorted.

SNORTING COCAINE

When a person is going to snort cocaine, he or she breathes it into the nose in the form of a fine, smooth powder. The cocaine is then absorbed into the bloodstream through the soft tissues inside the nasal passages.

Because the high is short-lived, the user snorts more and more cocaine, until the soft tissues inside the nose are swollen and numb. The more cocaine ingested, the more damage is done to these tissues.

Damage from Snorting

Cocaine is like a tornado, damaging everything in its path. Because cocaine acts as an anesthetic, the user doesn't usually feel much pain while snorting. In truth, however, as you snort more and more, your nose is getting severely damaged. Here are some of the painful—and pretty disgusting—things that happen to your nose when you use cocaine:

 First your nose feels stuffed up, as if you had a cold, and then it starts to run. This is because the cocaine seriously irritates your sinuses.

 After you snort cocaine several times, the inside of your nose will start to dry out. This makes it crack and bleed. You may also start to develop sores on your nose and upper lip.

Are you ready to be grossed out even more? In addicts who have used cocaine heavily, the drug actually starts to eat holes in the septum. Fixing these holes takes a lot more than a few Band-Aids. We're talking serious surgery here.

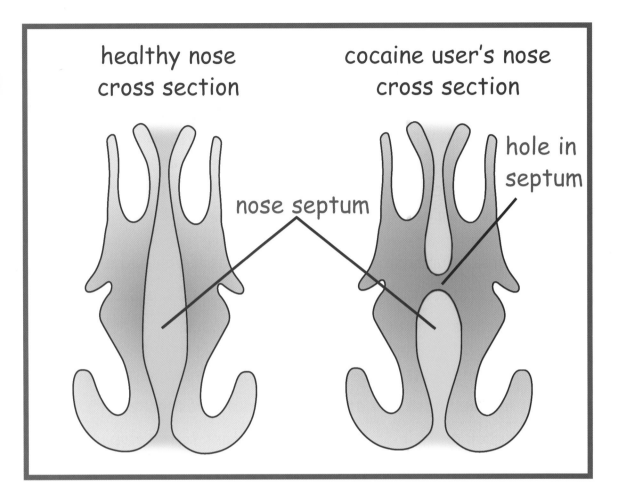

healthy nose
cross section

cocaine user's nose
cross section

hole in
septum

nose septum

Another serious side effect of cocaine on the nose is that it can completely ruin your sense of smell. This happens because cocaine makes the blood vessels in your nose constrict, or get smaller. Over time, this prevents blood from reaching your nose. When that happens, your nerve cells—and eventually the flesh in your nose—actually die, making your nose pretty much a dead organ.

A less obvious but really serious risk of snorting cocaine is catching dangerous diseases like hepatitis or HIV, the virus that causes AIDS. How can that happen from snorting? Well, as you know, people use straws (or rolled up pieces of paper) to inhale cocaine powder into their nose. Often these straws are passed around from user to user. Since cocaine users often have bloody noses or cracked skin, it's very easy for some of their blood to get on the straw. If an infected user gets blood on the straw and then passes the straw to other users who have cracked skin or sores, the infections can enter those users' bodies and make them sick.

You've learned that snorting cocaine can ruin your nose. It can cause you to lose your sense of smell and give you nosebleeds, sores, chronically stuffed-up sinuses, and an irritated and runny nose. Snorting cocaine can also affect your throat, making your voice hoarse, and may cause you difficulty in swallowing. But snorting cocaine is just one of the many dangerous and disgusting ways to ingest cocaine.

Smoking Cocaine

Smoking is another way people do cocaine. When people smoke cocaine, they use a different form of cocaine,

nose and lip sores

Infections, such as nose or lip sores, are often spread from one user to another through the sharing of cocaine straws.

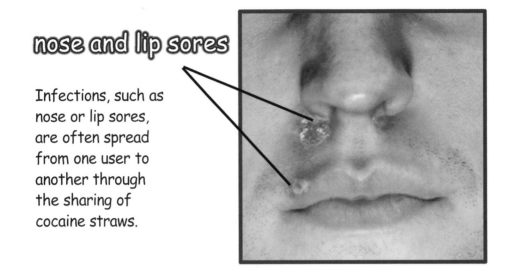

which is called crack. Crack cocaine is sometimes called freebase because it is the chemical base of cocaine. In other words, crack is a purer and, as a result, more powerful form of cocaine.

Because crack cocaine is dense and rocklike, it cannot be snorted or injected. It must be smoked. Once smoked, crack reaches the brain in about five seconds. A typical crack high is short-lived and lasts no longer than fifteen minutes. Crack is highly addictive. Because the effects of crack are strong yet brief, it is one of the most dangerous drugs you can take.

Crack is also extremely harmful to your body. Crack can cause terrible chest pain and breathing problems that don't go away. Just like snorting cocaine, smoking crack can cause dry lips, tongue, and throat, and can make your voice hoarse.

Smoking crack can do other damage, too. It can singe your eyebrows and eyelashes, and even burn your skin. In 1980, actor and comedian Richard Pryor suffered serious burns on more than half of his body from a bad accident while using crack.

Injecting Cocaine

The third way of doing cocaine is by injecting it into your veins with a needle. This method of doing cocaine gives the most powerful and dangerous high because it allows the drug to enter the bloodstream faster and in greater amounts.

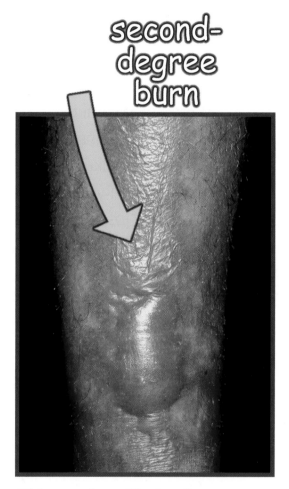

second-degree burn

This man is suffering from second-degree burns. This type of burn can result in shock so acute (severe) that the body's blood pressure will drop to a dangerously low level, possibly resulting in death.

Because injecting cocaine gives a person such an intense high and such a depressing low, users often mix cocaine with heroin when injecting. This mixture is called a speedball, and it is extremely deadly.

There are several risks a person takes when injecting cocaine. Injecting needles into your veins repeatedly causes irritation and can make your veins close up. When that happens, blood can't reach your arms, fingers, or other extremities, and you eventually lose control of these body parts. Can you imagine not being able to use your arms or legs?

When you inject cocaine, you put yourself at risk for several diseases, such as pneumonia, tuberculosis, and HIV. Any time you cannot verify that you are using a clean or unused needle, you are putting your life in serious danger. This is because even the tiniest drop of infected blood can pass disease to other human bodies.

HOW COCAINE AFFECTS YOUR BRAIN

Cocaine works on the part of your brain that makes you have strong feelings about things. People who use cocaine don't feel hungry or tired when they are high. Instead, they feel like they have a lot of strength, power, and energy. Sounds pretty good, doesn't it?

But cocaine also messes up the chemicals in your brain. By changing around these chemicals, cocaine makes you think that you want cocaine very badly and that it's a good and necessary thing. This feeling is called a craving. A craving is a very strong desire (want) for something. Have you ever really, really wanted chocolate or ice cream? Did you feel like you might just go nuts if you didn't get that food?

The craving probably went away after a while, either because you finally got the food or you were distracted by something else. Food cravings are normal and pretty harmless. But a cocaine craving can be dangerous because if you continue to satisfy the craving you may become addicted. When you are addicted to something, your body doesn't just want it badly anymore—now it needs that thing in order to just feel normal.

HOW COCAINE AFFECTS YOUR HEART

Your heart is responsible for pumping blood that is full of oxygen to all areas of your body. If your heart can't do its job, your body doesn't get the oxygen it needs to survive, and you die. In general, cocaine makes your heart beat faster than it should. Cocaine can also cause your blood to clot much faster than it normally would. If a

clogged vein

Cocaine use can cause the blood to clot abnormally fast, which can lead to a heart attack or stroke.

clot forms in one of the major passageways that carry blood to the heart, it can lead to a heart attack. This is why people who have never had any heart problems can die from a surprise heart attack, even after just one use of cocaine.

HOW COCAINE AFFECTS THE REST OF YOUR BODY

Have you ever heard someone say something like "your body is your temple"? Of course, this doesn't mean that your body is a kind of building. But like a temple, your body is sacred and should be treated with respect. You get only one body in your lifetime, and how you treat it and take care of it when you are young has a lot to do with how long it will last. Using cocaine can cause damage all over your body. Once these body parts are ruined, there's usually no repairing them. And your body can't function for long with damaged parts.

What are we trying to say here? Let's get to the point. These are the facts: cocaine can harm your heart, brain, blood vessels, lungs, throat, and, of course, your nose. If any one of these systems becomes too damaged, you will die.

COCAINE AND WITHDRAWAL

If someone who is addicted to cocaine suddenly stops using the drug, he or she will experience withdrawal, or "coming down." This is a very painful process that happens with many different drugs.

The happy feeling that the cocaine caused at first goes away and the person ends up feeling really, really sick. People going through withdrawal often feel hungry, irritable (crabby), apathetic (not caring what happens), depressed (very down and blue), and paranoid (worried that everyone is out to get them).

That's not all. Users in withdrawal have intense cravings, think a lot about committing suicide, lose interest in sex, and suffer from serious sleeping problems like insomnia (not being able to sleep) or sleeping too much. They also probably have some stomach problems like diarrhea or constipation.

One of the scariest symptoms of cocaine withdrawal is hallucinations, which can occur after constant use. When you hallucinate, you think you see or hear something that isn't really there. People in cocaine withdrawal may imagine that there are snakes, worms, or bugs crawling on their bodies. They may even believe they can feel these creepy crawlies on their skin.

Some withdrawal symptoms last for only a few days. Others can stick around for longer. The worst part of withdrawal is that lots of times users don't have anyone to help them get through the painful process and they lose the willpower to quit drugs. Instead of sticking it out, they start taking cocaine again to make the bad feelings of withdrawal go away.

After you use cocaine regularly for a while, it really gets into your system and starts to damage things all over your body. Here are some bad effects of using cocaine: headaches, blurry or fuzzy vision, seeing spots, coughing, breathing problems, seizures, lung damage, overdose, and death.

COCAINE AND YOUR CASH

Some people say that cocaine users "snort all their money away" or that "all of their money goes right up their nose." As weird as those phrases may sound, they're pretty accurate. Buying enough cocaine to satisfy an addiction can cost you from hundreds to thousands of dollars every week. Spending all your money on cocaine will leave you broke and maybe even homeless.

5 Keeping Clean

As one of the main entrances to your respiratory system—the system in charge of the all-important job of breathing to keep you alive—your nose is a vital part of your body that must be kept healthy. Becoming addicted to cocaine is the easy part—most of the time it happens before you even know it. Beating the addiction may be the hardest thing you will ever do, but thousands of people do it every year.

There are many organizations out there that want to help addicts get over their drug habit. For information and support, contact some of the sources listed in the back of this book.

GET SOME HELP

For many people who are addicted to cocaine, the hardest part of getting over the addiction is admitting that they have a problem in the first place. Some people are too proud to admit it, and other people are just too embarrassed. But the fact is, if you don't admit your problem and you don't get help, cocaine will mess up your nose, the rest of your body, and eventually your whole life.

For those of you who are reading this book because you think someone you know may have a problem with cocaine, you may be able to save that person's life by sharing this information with him or her. It can be very difficult to talk to someone about a drug problem, but it doesn't pay to be shy when it comes to the dangers of drugs. Contact the places listed in this book for advice about how to protect yourself and those around you.

GLOSSARY

addiction The physical and/or psychological need for a drug in order to get through each day and feel normal.

anesthetic A painkilling drug that causes loss of feeling or consciousness.

cartilage Elastic tissue that makes up the long part of the nose (along with bone) and connects the nose to the skull.

craving An intense and urgent need for a drug.

pharynx The throat.

respiration The process of breathing in oxygen and breathing out carbon dioxide.

respiratory system The set of organs, including the nose, mouth, and lungs, that enables you to breathe.

seizure A sudden attack or convulsion, usually due to a physical disorder or to drug use.

septum A wall made of cartilage and bone that divides the nose.

FOR MORE INFORMATION

Hotlines

Girls and Boys Town National
Hotline (800) 448-3000

National Drug and Alcohol
Treatment Referral Service
(800) 662-HELP (662-4357)

Drughelp.org
(800) HELP 111 (435-7111)

The National Youth Crisis Hotline
(800) HIT HOME (448-4663)

Organizations

Narcotics Anonymous
P.O. Box 9999
Van Nuys, CA 91409
(818) 773-9999
Web site: http://www.na.org

National Clearinghouse for
Alcohol & Drug Information
P.O. Box 2345

Rockville, MD 20847-2345
(800) 729-6686
Web site: http://www.health.org

National Council on Alcoholism
and Drug Dependence
20 Exchange Place, Suite 2902
New York, NY 10005
(800) NCA-CALL [622-2255]
e-mail: national@ncadd.org
Web site: http://www.ncadd.org

Web Sites

Due to the changing nature of
Internet links, the Rosen
Publishing Group, Inc., has developed an online list of Web sites
related to the subject of this
book. This site is updated regularly. Please use this link to access
the list:

http://www.rosenlinks.com/
idd/cono

FOR FURTHER READING

Aretha, David. *Cocaine and Crack (Drugs)*. Berkeley Heights, NJ: Enslow Publishers, Inc., 2005.

Landau, Elaine. *Cocaine* (Watts Library: Human Health and Disease). New York: Franklin Watts, 2003.

Nagle, Jeanne M. *Everything You Need to Know About Drug Addiction* (Need to Know Library). New York: Rosen Publishing Group, 1999.

Robbins, Paul R. *Crack and Cocaine (Drug Dangers)*. Berkeley Heights, NJ: Enslow Publishers, 1999.

Turck, Mary C., and Laurie Beckleman. *Crack and Cocaine (Facts About)*. Parsippany, NJ: Silver Burdett Press, 1999.

INDEX

About the Author

Melanie Apel is a pediatric respiratory therapist at the Children's Memorial Hospital in Chicago. She has a degree in respiratory care from National-Louis University and a degree in theater arts from Bradley University. Her other books for the Rosen Publishing Group include *Drug Interactions*, as well as twelve titles in the PowerKids Press Let's Talk Library series. When she is not writing, Melanie likes to figure skate, travel, and spend time with loved ones.

Photo Credits